📖 SCHOLASTIC

National Curric

ENGLISH

Revision Guide

✓ Recap
✓ Revise
✓ Skills Check

Ages 8–9
Year 4

KS2

SCHOLASTIC

National Curriculum
ENGLISH
Revision Guide

Book End, Range Road, Witney, Oxfordshire, OX29 0YD
Registered office: Westfield Road, Southam, Warwickshire CV47 0RA
www.scholastic.co.uk

© 2016, Scholastic Ltd

2 3 4 5 6 7 8 9   6 7 8 9 0 1 2 3 4 5

British Library Cataloguing-in-Publication Data
A catalogue record for this book is available from the British Library.

ISBN 978-1407-15980-5
Printed by Bell & Bain Ltd, Glasgow

Author
Catherine Casey

Consultants
Lesley and Graham Fletcher

Editorial
Rachel Morgan, Tracey Cowell, Maggie Donovan, Shelley Welsh and Helen Lewis

Series Design
Scholastic Design Team: Nicolle Thomas and Neil Salt

Design
Oxford Designers & Illustrators

Cover Design
Scholastic Design Team: Nicolle Thomas and Neil Salt

Cover Illustration
Shutterstock / © VIGE.CO

Illustration
Simon Walmesley

Contents

Using the revision guide

From 2016 new-style National Curriculum Tests will be introduced for children at the end of Key Stage 1 (7 years old) and at the end of Key Stage 2 (11 years old). Children will take tests in Grammar, Punctuation and Spelling, and Reading.

• These books are written by teachers for the National Curriculum to help children revise for end-of-year school tests in Grammar, Punctuation and Spelling, and Reading.

• Each book is split into five sections, which match the content to be covered by the tests.

• Revising for the tests will help children feel prepared and prevent them from worrying about the unknown.

• Use the books to practise skills 'little and often'. Don't attempt to do too much in one session.

• At the back of the book is a **revision planner** to enable you to record what content has been covered and to prioritise what still needs to be done.

• Year 3, 4 and 5 tests are not compulsory but the Revision Books will help children preparing for assessments and tests in school.

• A series of **Practice Tests** is available to help children towards the next stage of their preparations for National and school tests.

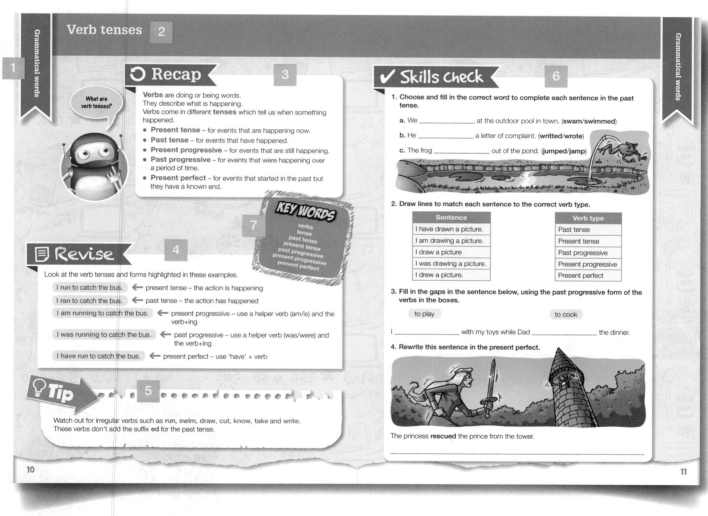

1 Chapter title

2 Subject title

3 Each page starts with a **recap** and a 'What is...' question which gives children a clear definition for the terminology used.

4 In the **revise** section there are clear teaching examples, using fun characters and clear illustrations and diagrams.

5 **Tips** are included to help show important points to remember and to give helpful strategies for remembering.

6 The **skills check** sections enable children to practise what they have learned using National Test-style questions.

7 **Key words** that children need to know are displayed. Definitions for these words can be found in the **Glossary**.

Proper nouns and common nouns

What are proper nouns and common nouns?

↻ Recap

Nouns are the names of people, places and things. There are different types of noun.

A **proper noun** names something specific and a **common noun** names something in general.

Revise

In this table, the nouns have been sorted into common nouns and proper nouns.

Common noun	Proper noun
month	August
planet	Saturn
building	Eiffel Tower

Look at the nouns highlighted in this example.

Jack travelled to France on an aeroplane.

↑ proper noun (name of specific person)

↑ proper noun (name of specific place)

↑ common noun (name of thing)

Tip

Remember, proper nouns always start with a capital letter.

Can you find the nouns in these sentences?

✔ Skills Check

1. **Underline the common nouns and circle the proper nouns in these sentences.**

   a. The astronauts prepared for their journey to Mars.

   b. Ms Green gave the class their homework.

   c. The doctor used a stethoscope to listen to Amelia's heart.

   d. The tourists visited Buckingham Palace in London.

   e. "My birthday is in June," said Hannah excitedly.

KEY WORDS

nouns
proper nouns
common nouns

Adjectives

What is an adjective?

⟳ Recap

Adjectives are often called describing words. They describe features of nouns such as colour, age, shape or size.

📄 Revise

Look at the adjectives highlighted in this example. They give us more detail about the lighthouse steps.

What effect do different adjectives have on the sentence?

The **ancient** lighthouse steps were **creaky** and **rotten**.

Tip 💡

Adjectives make a sentence more interesting by providing the reader with more detail.

KEY WORDS

adjectives

✔ Skills Check

1. **Improve these sentences by using more exciting adjectives than the ones in bold.**

   a. The (**big**) _____ fish swam around the pond.

   b. The captain climbed aboard the (**old**) _____ boat.

   c. The sandwiches we ate for lunch were (**nice**) _____.

2. **Rewrite these sentences, adding adjectives to make them more interesting.**

   a. The owl sat on a branch.

   _____

   b. The cyclist rode down the lane.

   _____

   c. The teacher entered the hall.

   _____

Adjectives with prefixes

↻ Recap

How do prefixes change adjectives?

A **prefix** is a set of letters added to the beginning of a word. When prefixes are added to adjectives, they can change their meaning.

📄 Revise

Let's look at the prefixes in these examples and see how they change the meaning of the adjective they are added to.

Prefix	Adjective	New word
un	happy	unhappy
in	active	inactive
im	polite	impolite
ir	regular	irregular

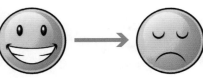

The prefixes un, in, im and ir give the adjective the opposite meaning.

✔ Skills Check

1. Add the prefix to the adjective to create a new word. Write the new word in the box.

Prefix	Adjective	New word
un	helpful	
in	complete	
ir	responsible	

KEY WORD

prefix

2. What effect does the prefix 'un' have on these words? Explain your answer.

un + interested = **un**interested   **un** + safe = **un**safe

_____

_____

_____

_____

Tip 💡

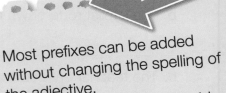

Most prefixes can be added without changing the spelling of the adjective.
For example: **un** + comfortable = **un**comfortable

Noun phrases

What is a noun phrase?

↻ Recap

A **noun phrase** has a noun as its main word and has one or more adjectives and/or a preposition (see page 22).

📋 Revise

Let's look at the expanded noun phrases highlighted in these examples.

The **amazing new robot with three arms** cleaned the floor!

↗ adjectives ↗ noun ↖ preposition ↖ noun

I bought **the last computer-tablet in the shop**.

↗ adjective ↗ noun ↖ preposition ↖ noun

The swimmer dived into **the cold outdoor pool behind the trees**.

↗ adjectives ↗ noun ↖ preposition ↖ noun

You know about adjectives, but can you see how to use prepositions to give more information?

✔ Skills check

1. **Underline the noun phrases in these sentences.**

   a. The lonely, frightened evacuee with a suitcase stood on the platform.

   b. The robin stood on the broken, empty bird-bath by the path.

   c. The children played happily in the soft, yellow sand near the dunes.

   d. Amber borrowed the only English dictionary in the library.

   e. Omar took the last apple muffin on the tray.

KEY WORD

noun phrases

Verb tenses

↻ Recap

What are verb tenses?

Verbs are doing or being words.
They describe what is happening.
Verbs come in different **tenses** which tell us when something happened.

- **Present tense** – for events that are happening now.
- **Past tense** – for events that have happened.
- **Present progressive** – for events that are still happening.
- **Past progressive** – for events that were happening over a period of time.
- **Present perfect** – for events that started in the past but they have a known end.

KEY WORDS

verbs
tense
past tense
present tense
past progressive
present progressive
present perfect

📝 Revise

Look at the verb tenses and forms highlighted in these examples.

I **run** to catch the bus. ⬅ present tense – the action is happening

I **ran** to catch the bus. ⬅ past tense – the action has happened

I **am running** to catch the bus. ⬅ present progressive – use a helper verb (am/is) and the verb+ing

I **was running** to catch the bus. ⬅ past progressive – use a helper verb (was/were) and the verb+ing

I **have run** to catch the bus. ⬅ present perfect – use 'have' + verb

💡 Tip

Watch out for irregular verbs such as **run**, **swim**, **draw**, **cut**, **know**, **take** and **write**.
These verbs don't add the suffix **ed** for the past tense.

✔ Skills Check

1. Choose and fill in the correct word to complete each sentence in the past tense.

  a. We _____ at the outdoor pool in town. (**swam/swimmed**)

  b. He _____ a letter of complaint. (**writted/wrote**)

  c. The frog _____ out of the pond. (**jumped/jamp**)

2. Draw lines to match each sentence to the correct verb type.

Sentence
I have drawn a picture.
I am drawing a picture.
I draw a picture
I was drawing a picture.
I drew a picture.

Verb type
Past tense
Present tense
Past progressive
Present progressive
Present perfect

3. Fill in the gaps in the sentence below, using the past progressive form of the verbs in the boxes.

  to play   to cook

I _____ with my toys while Dad _____ the dinner.

4. Rewrite this sentence in the present perfect.

The princess **rescued** the prince from the tower.

_____

Adverbs

What is an adverb?

↺ Recap

Adverbs describe verbs. They tell you more about the event or action, describing how, when, where or why something happens.

📄 Revise

Here are some different types of adverb.

How something happens	When or how often something happens	Where something happens	Why something happens
unexpectedly	today	here	therefore
powerfully	now	there	otherwise
accidentally	soon	everywhere	consequently
gracefully	never	indoors	hence
mysteriously	often	upstairs	
gradually	regularly	abroad	

Look at the **adverbs** highlighted in these examples and how they describe the **verb**.

Mysteriously, my socks have **disappeared**. ← describes how the socks have disappeared

I **go** swimming **regularly**. ← describes how often I go swimming

They **looked everywhere** for the ball. ← describes where they looked

💡 Tip

Adverbs can be at the beginning, middle or end of a sentence.

KEY WORD

adverbs

✔ Skills Check

1. Circle the adverb in each sentence below.

   a. Sadly, James picked up the broken doll.

   b. We sometimes play tennis.

   c. The children are playing downstairs.

   d. I went shopping yesterday.

   e. Suddenly, the cat leapt off the wall.

2. Complete these sentences with a suitable adverb.

   a. _____, the children splashed in the paddling pool together.

   b. The dog barked _____ .

   c. _____, I am going to the cinema.

   d. The cat curled up _____ after a night hunting mice.

   e. _____, the dentist removed the tooth.

3. Replace the adverbs that are underlined in the sentences below.
Rewrite each sentence.

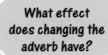

> **What effect does changing the adverb have?**

   a. Flora broke the precious glass <u>accidentally</u>.

_____

   b. Nikhil was playing <u>indoors</u>, with the ball.

_____

   c. <u>Often</u>, I get the bus to school.

_____

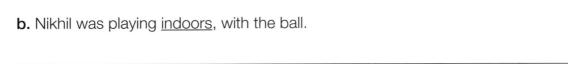

Adverbials

What is an adverbial?

↺ Recap

An **adverbial** is a group of words or a phrase that behaves like an adverb. It tells you more about the event or action such as how, when, where or why.

📄 Revise

These two examples show how adverbs and adverbials do the same 'job' in a sentence.

> I **go** swimming **regularly**.
>
> ↑
>
> **adverb** describes how often I go swimming

> I **go** swimming **every Monday and Thursday**.
>
> ↑
>
> **adverbial** describes how often I go swimming

Look at the different types of adverbial highlighted in these examples.

> Isabel **ate** her dinner **as slowly as she could**.
>
> ↑
>
> adverbial: tells you how Isabel ate

> The cricket team **had** oranges **at half time**.
>
> ↑
>
> adverbial: tells you when the cricket team had oranges

> We **had** a barbeque **on the patio**.
>
> ↑
>
> adverbial: tells you where we had a barbeque

> The mouse **fled because of the cat**.
>
> ↑
>
> adverbial: tells you why the mouse fled

✔ Skills Check

1. **Underline the adverbial in each sentence below.**

   a. I went to the park last Thursday afternoon.

   b. We waited for our drinks in the sunshine.

   c. The little girl ran to the finishing line as fast as she could.

   d. The children were playing football all morning.

   e. The enormous dog barked in the garden.

KEY WORD

adverbials

14

Fronted adverbials

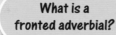

↺ Recap

What is a fronted adverbial?

Fronted adverbials are adverbials that are at the beginning of a sentence.

📄 Revise

Let's see how the adverbials highlighted in these examples can move to the front of the sentence. Fronted adverbials are usually followed by a comma.

The baby slept **in his cot**.   **In his cot**, the baby slept.

      ↑   ↑   ↖

     adverbial   fronted adverbial   comma

both describe where the baby slept

We went bowling **the day before yesterday**.

↑

adverbial

The day before yesterday, we went bowling.

↑   ↑

fronted adverbial   comma

both describe when they went bowling

KEY WORD

fronted adverbials

✔ Skills check

1. **Rewrite the sentences below so that they begin with the adverbial in bold. Use only the same words.**

   a. Ms Wilkinson played the piano **in assembly**.

   _____

   b. The bell rang **suddenly**.

   _____

   c. We went inside **at the end of break time**.

   _____

   d. The woman walked her dog **along the beach**.

   _____

Clauses

What is a clause?

↻ Recap

A **clause** is a group of words that contains a verb and tell you who or what is doing the verb. Clauses can sometimes be complete sentences.

- A **main clause** makes sense on its own, tells you who or what does the verb and has a verb.
- A **subordinate clause** needs the rest of the sentence (a main clause) to make sense. A subordinate clause includes a conjunction to link it to the main clause.

📄 Revise

Look at the main and subordinate clauses highlighted in these examples. A main clause can be a sentence on its own.

She is going out.
↑
main clause

She is going out **after** she has eaten her dinner.
↑   ↑   ↑
main clause –   conjunction   subordinate clause
makes sense   – does not make
by itself   sense by itself

When I picked it up, the hamster tickled my hands.
↑   ↑   ↑
conjunction   subordinate   main clause –
                   clause – does   makes sense
                   not make sense   by itself
                   by itself

KEY WORDS
clause
main clause
subordinate clause

💡 Tips

Subordinate clauses can be at the beginning or end of a sentence.

Can you tell if these clauses are main clauses or subordinate clauses?

✔ Skills Check

1. **Put a tick in each row to show whether the main clause or the subordinate clause is in bold.**

	Main clause	Subordinate clause
I washed my hands **after I went to the toilet**.		
When I lost my favourite teddy, I was upset.		
I jumped when the door slammed loudly.		
Before I went on stage, **I was feeling nervous**.		
I shut the window when it rained.		
The lights went out **because the power was cut off**.		

2. **Underline the main clause in each sentence below.**

   a. The girl walked to school although it was raining.

   b. The bus was late because it broke down.

   c. As it was snowing, the football match was cancelled.

3. **Underline the subordinate clause in each sentence below.**

   a. He cleaned out the guinea pigs after feeding the rabbit.

   b. When we were younger, we went ice-skating with our grandma.

   c. If I go on Saturday, I will see the animals at the zoo.

Conjunctions

What is a conjunction?

↻ Recap

Conjunctions join words or clauses together.
- **Co-ordinating conjunctions** link two main clauses together. They include: **and**   **but**   **or**   **so**
- **Subordinating conjunctions** link a subordinate clause to a main clause. They include: **when**   **if**   **after**   **because**   **before**

📋 Revise

Look at the co-ordinating and subordinating conjunctions highlighted in these examples.

I enjoy swimming **but** I don't like diving.

↑	↑	↑
main clause	**co-ordinating conjunction**	main clause

She went to the park **because** she wanted to go on the swings.

↑	↑	↑
main clause	**subordinating conjunction**	subordinate clause

When you knocked on the door, I opened it.

↑	↑	↑
subordinating conjunction	subordinate clause	main clause

KEY WORDS

conjunctions
co-ordinating conjunctions
subordinating conjunctions

✔ Skills Check

1. **Circle the co-ordinating conjunctions and underline the subordinating conjunctions in the sentences below.**

   a. She put sun cream on before she went outside.

   b. I have two brothers so I know lots about football.

   c. You can have raisins or you can have grapes.

   d. If you cook dinner, I'll do the washing up.

Determiners

Speech bubble: What is a determiner?

↻ Recap

Determiners go before a noun (or noun phrase) and show which noun you are talking about. They can tell you whether the noun is known or unknown, who it belongs to or how many there are. Determiners

include: **the**   **a**   **an**   **your**   **my**   **some**   **every**

📋 Revise

KEY WORD
determiners

Determiners tell you…	Examples	Sentences
whether the noun is known or not	**a** or **an** (unknown) **the** (known)	I saw **an** umbrella lying in the corridor. **The** umbrella was blue.
who the noun belongs to	**your, my, their, her**	Can I borrow **your** coat? **My** coat is still wet.
how many of the noun	**some, every, one, two**	**Some** children forgot their homework. **Two** cats were sitting on the wall.

Here are some examples of determiners in use.

💡 **Tip**

"Can you get me **a** new library **book**?" asked Thomas.

determiner: **a** (an unknown noun – could be any book)

determiner

"They've got **some** great books on wizards!" enthused Arthur.
"**My** favourite one is **the book** on Italian cooking."

determiner

determiner: **the** (a known noun – Italian cooking book)

When you're using a/an:
- use **a** if the noun (or noun phrase) begins with a consonant
- use **an** if the noun (or noun phrase) begins with a vowel.

✔ Skills Check

1. Circle the determiner in each sentence below.

a. I need to see a dentist.   **b.** Please put on your socks and shoes.

2. Write the correct determiner to complete these sentences – a, an or some.

a. The boy ate _____ orange for his lunch.   **b.** Please can I have _____ peas?

Pronouns

What is a pronoun?

Pronouns are words used instead of nouns or noun phrases. It means that the noun does not need to be repeated.

📄 Revise

Pronouns replace nouns to avoid repetition. They include:

> I   she   he   it   you   we   they

Noun	Pronoun
Amira was late for school. **Amira** ran down the road.	Amira was late for school. **She** ran down the road.
The children were in the garden. **The children** were playing football.	The children were in the garden. **They** were playing football.

Possessive pronouns are used to show who or what something belongs to. They include:

> mine   hers   his   its   yours   ours   theirs

Noun	Pronoun
The teacher put on **the teacher's** jacket.	The teacher put on **his** jacket.
That book is **Mrs Newley's**.	That book is **hers**.
The cat has drunk all **the cat's** milk.	The cat has drunk all **its** milk.

💡 Tip

Be careful when you use pronouns – make sure it's clear which noun they refer to.

KEY WORDS

pronouns
possessive pronouns

✔ Skills Check

1. **Circle all the pronouns in the sentences below.**

   a. Ruby and Edward went to the park. They played football.

   b. I played the guitar loudly.

   c. Connor finished his homework quickly.

   d. Sarah was doing well at swimming. She didn't need her armbands any more.

   e. Darcy had PE but she couldn't find her kit.

2. **Complete the sentences by filling in the missing pronouns.**

   his   its   she   they   he

   a. Meesha was going to a party but _____ didn't like her dress.

   b. Felix was hungry because _____ had forgotten his packed lunch.

   c. The alien landed _____ spacecraft on the planet Earth.

   d. David and Rosie put on sun cream but _____ didn't wear their sun hats.

   e. Vishal searched everywhere but _____ couldn't

      find _____ school shoes.

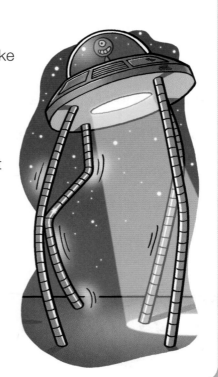

Prepositions

What is a preposition?

↺ Recap

Prepositions link nouns, pronouns or noun phrases to other words in the sentence.

Prepositions usually tell you about place, direction or time. They include:

before   after   during   in   because of

under   on   around   beside

📄 Revise

Look at the prepositions highlighted in these examples.

I wanted the shiny green scooter **in** the shop window.

Can I sleep **on** the top bunk bed?

I ran **around** the corner.

✔ Skills Check

1. **Circle the prepositions in these sentences.**

   a. We swam after lunch.

   b. I needed the toilet during assembly.

   c. The astronaut landed beside a crater.

   d. The lorry went under the bridge.

2. **Choose and fill in the best preposition to complete each sentence below.**

   a. School was closed _____ the snow. (**because of/on**)

   b. I had to eat all my carrots _____ pudding. (**in/before**)

   c. The snake was curled _____ a branch of the tree. (**around/after**)

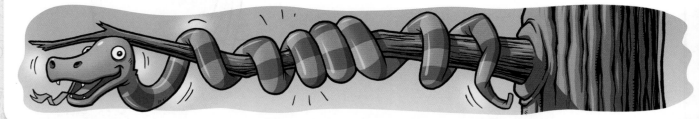

Capital letters

When do you use a capital letter?

↻ Recap

Use a capital letter:
- to mark the beginning of a sentence
- for proper nouns, including people's names, days of the week and names of places (such as cities, restaurants and shops).

▤ Revise

Look at the capital letters highlighted in this example.

The French chef rustled up a delicious lunch for Andrew.

to show the beginning of a sentence

to show proper nouns (nationality and a boy's name)

Tip

Remember to use a capital letter for the pronoun 'I'.

✔ Skills check

1. **Rewrite these sentences, putting capital letters in the correct places.**

   a. usually in october, the leaves fall off the trees.

   _____

   b. lily and meg visited edinburgh castle, on their school trip.

   _____

   c. the new pilot, who was called tom, often flew to germany.

   _____

2. **Elijah says, "Capital letters are only used at the beginning of a sentence."**

   Is he right? Circle the correct answer.   Yes   No

   Explain your answer.

   _____

Full stops, question marks and exclamation marks

When do you use a full stop, question mark or exclamation mark?

↻ Recap

Full stops mark the end of statements or commands.

Question marks show the end of questions.

Exclamation marks can be used to show strong feelings such as surprise or panic. They can also be used to indicate that someone is shouting or that something is very loud.

- . full stop
- ? question mark
- ! exclamation mark

🗒 Revise

"What fantastic writing today(!)" exclaimed Ms Black.

exclamation mark: to show the teacher's strong feelings about how well Lucy has done

"Really(?)" asked Lucy, wide-eyed.

question mark: to show Lucy is asking a question

"Yes, all the letters are joined clearly," replied Mrs Black, smiling(.)

full stop: to show the end of a sentence

KEY WORDS

full stops
question marks
exclamation marks

💡 Tips

- Full stops, question marks and exclamation marks help the reader to use the correct expression and emphasis when reading.
- Exclamation marks are often used when writing direct speech.

✔ Skills Check

1. a. Which sentence is punctuated most appropriately? Tick one.

When it rains, our garden is full of puddles. ☐

When it rains, our garden is full of puddles! ☐

When it rains, our garden is full of puddles? ☐

b. Explain your answer.

_____

_____

2. Complete each sentence with the most appropriate punctuation mark.

a. When can I go outside to play ◯

b. When it rains hard, we have break time inside ◯

c. Pick that up ◯

d. What an amazing feeling ◯

3. In the passage below, some of the punctuation is missing. Add the correct punctuation in each of the spaces.

. ! ?

It was the school holidays ◯ Jessica and Nathan were out walking in the woods when they came to a broken bridge.
"How annoying ◯ " cried Nathan.
"How are we going to get across the stream now ◯ " thought Jessica.
They both looked at the fast-flowing stream and the slippy rocks underneath the broken bridge ◯ It was no good, they would have to walk downstream until they found a safe place to cross.

Apostrophes for contraction

↻ Recap

What is an apostrophe for contraction?

An **apostrophe** is a punctuation mark: '

Apostrophes for **contraction** are used to show the place of a missing letter or letters when two words are joined (for example, **that's** for **that is**).

目 Revise

Look at the examples. The apostrophe goes where the missing letters are.

Words in full	Contraction	Sentence
it is	**it's**	**It's** a long way to Grandad's house.
they are	**they're**	**They're** going to win the race.
could not	**couldn't**	She **couldn't** reach the top shelf.
he will	**he'll**	**He'll** have to look in the lost property box.
I have	**I've**	**I've** finished my work.
what is	**what's**	**What's** the time?
you are	**you're**	**You're** swimming in the main pool tonight.

💡 Tip

When you see a contraction, think about what it *means*, so you can work out what the missing letters are.

✔ Skills Check

KEY WORDS
apostrophes
contraction

1. Rewrite these words as contractions using an apostrophe.

| does not | | He is |

a. He _____ want to go to school today. _____ unwell.

| cannot | | I will |

b. I _____ remember my password. _____ have to reset it.

2. Rewrite these contractions in full.

Words in full	Contraction	Words in full	Contraction
	you'd		should've
	aren't		he'll

Apostrophes for possession

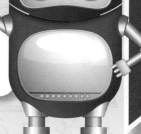

What is an apostrophe for possession?

↻ Recap

Apostrophes for **possession** show who or what something belongs to.

📋 Revise

If something belongs to one person then you add **'s**.

> I borrowed **Tracey's umbrella** to go out in the rain.
>
>
>
> shows that the umbrella belonged to Tracey

Who do the items belong to in these sentences?

If it is an irregular plural that doesn't end with **s**, then add **'s**.

> The cloakroom was a mess because the **children's coats** were all over the floor.
>
> ↑
>
> shows that the coats belonged to the children

If something belongs to more than one person then you add an apostrophe after the s.

> It was the **girls' turn** to go on the trampoline.
>
>
>
> shows that the turn belonged to the girls (plural – more than one girl)

✔ Skills check

1. **Circle the word in each sentence that should contain an apostrophe. Then rewrite it in the box to show that there is more than one owner in each case.**

   a. After PE, the childrens school shoes were all muddled up. [ ]

   b. The bridesmaids dresses had not arrived. [ ]

   c. The babies mouths were wide open in surprise. [ ]

   d. All the boys costumes were ready. [ ]

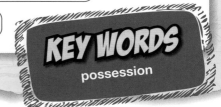

KEY WORDS

possession

Inverted commas

What are inverted commas?

↺ Recap

Inverted commas are punctuation marks that show **direct speech**: " "

Sometimes they are also called speech marks.

📄 Revise

Inverted commas go at the beginning and end of direct speech. They enclose the spoken words and the punctuation that goes with the speech. Who is talking and how comes outside of the inverted commas.

"Tomorrow I'm going to my friend's house," said Sophia.

↑ inverted commas   ↑ direct speech   ↑ final comma: inside the inverted commas   ↑ who is talking and how

Tomorrow I'm going to my friend's house.

"Which way is the post office, please?" asked the old man.

↑ inverted commas   ↑ question mark: inside the inverted commas

Which way is the post office, please?

"I'm over here!" shouted Jakub.

↑ inverted commas   ↑ exclamation mark: inside the inverted commas

I'm over here!

The teacher told the children, **"Line up now."**

↑ who is talking and how first, followed by a comma: before the inverted commas   ↑ comma   ↑ inverted commas

Line up now.

Tips

- Use a comma after who is talking, when it comes before the direct speech.
- When you're writing down a conversation, start a new line each time the speaker changes.

KEY WORDS
inverted commas
direct speech

✔ **Skills Check**

1. Which sentence uses inverted commas correctly? Tick one.

"Look at all that rain"! exclaimed Grandad. "I think we will have to go in the car today". ☐

"Look at all that rain! exclaimed Grandad. I think we will have to go in the car today." ☐

"Look at all that rain!" exclaimed Grandad. "I think we will have to go in the car today." ☐

"Look at all that rain!" exclaimed Grandad. "I think we will have to go in the car today". ☐

2. In the passage below, insert the missing inverted commas.

Charlie was standing at the end of the dinner queue.

I am so hungry! he moaned.

Me too. Why are we always last? said his friend Sam.

I just hope there is some chocolate cake left, replied Jing, who was just
in front of Charlie.

Then the lunchtime assistant told them, You don't need to worry. There's
plenty of cake for everyone.

Commas in lists

When and how do you use commas in a list?

↻ Recap

Commas can be used to separate items in a list instead of repeating the word 'and'.

🗐 Revise

You put a comma between each item in the list except the last item, where you use 'and'. An item in a list may be a single word or several words.

Look at these examples to see how it's done.

> At the school fete there was a **bouncy castle, cake stalls, live music and some games.**

> For lunch I had **delicious sandwiches, a bunch of green grapes and the very last biscuit.**

💡 Tip

You don't need to use a comma if there are only two words in the list.
For example: The boy had a football and a lunchbox.

✔ Skills Check

1. Which sentence uses commas in a list correctly? Tick one.

He used, flour, sugar, butter and eggs to make a delicious cake. ☐

He used flour, sugar, butter and eggs to make a delicious cake. ☐

He used flour, sugar, butter, eggs to make a delicious cake. ☐

He used flour, sugar, butter, and eggs to make a delicious cake. ☐

2. Insert the missing commas to complete these sentences.

a. For breakfast, I had pancakes yoghurt fruit and honey.

b. On sports day, she competed in the egg and spoon race the skipping race and the obstacle race.

c. In the film about nocturnal animals there were owls bats and foxes.

KEY WORD

commas

30

Commas after fronted adverbials

↻ Recap

What are commas after fronted adverbials?

A **fronted adverbial** is an adverbial placed at the beginning of a sentence. It is usually followed by a comma.

An adverbial tells you how, when, where or why.

▤ Revise

Look at the fronted adverbials and commas highlighted in these examples.

In assembly, I played the recorder.

↑ fronted adverbial   ↖ comma

After break time, he had a French lesson.

↑ fronted adverbial   ↖ comma

Tomorrow morning, we are going on holiday.

↑ fronted adverbial   ↖ comma

✔ Skills Check

1. **Add a comma in the correct place to the sentences below.**

   a. Before school I had a swimming lesson.

   b. Last year my teacher was Mr Davies.

   c. At the weekend her aunt came to visit.

KEY WORD
fronted adverbials

2. **Rewrite each sentence below so that it begins with the adverbial. Use only the same words. Don't forget the comma.**

   a. It snowed and snowed in January.

   _____

   b. I went to the museum yesterday afternoon.

   _____

   c. We had to sit and wait at the airport for Granny's plane.

   _____

Paragraphs

What is a paragraph?

↺ Recap

A paragraph is a group of sentences about the same topic. Paragraphs make text easier to read by breaking it into smaller sections. They are used to organise ideas around a common theme.

📄 Revise

A new paragraph should start when the topic changes. The first sentence of each paragraph should indicate what the paragraph is about. For example, look at the paragraphs in the passage below.

💡 Tip

You can use pronouns within and across paragraphs to link information together without repeating the noun. Make sure it's clear which noun you're referring to.

Pond dipping

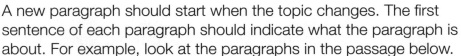

On Wednesday, **Class 6** went pond dipping. We had to walk up to the pond which was along a main road. Mr Hall put us into pairs and gave us reflective jackets to wear to keep us safe. I was excited about the creatures we might find. We had been learning about habitats in Science lessons.

← **first paragraph**: about the journey

We needed lots of special equipment for pond dipping. We used strong dip nets to catch the wildlife, white trays to put our catches in so we could see any creatures easily, magnifying glasses to look at the creatures carefully and charts to identify the insects.

← the pronoun **we** refers to **Class 6** in the previous paragraph

← **second paragraph**: about the equipment

I caught a tadpole which had two legs. There was also frog spawn in the pond. The frog spawn looked like little balls of white jelly with tiny black dots inside. Mr Hall told us that tadpoles develop tiny teeth! My tadpole had two legs so was probably about 9 weeks old.

← first sentence tells you what the paragraph is about

← **third paragraph**: about the tadpole caught during pond dipping

✔ Skills Check

1. Read this passage and then answer the questions below.

Then I saw a huge dragonfly high up above the water. It was much bigger than I expected. Dragonflies can be beautiful colours. The one we spotted by the pond was blue and dark green. It had enormous eyes that covered the whole of its head. After that, I stuck the dip net right to the very bottom of the pond. I got my coat a bit wet but I caught some flatworms. Flatworms live on the bottom of the pond, which I already knew because we learned about it in class. When we had looked at the creatures with our magnifying glasses, we did sketches and labelled them. Mr Hall made us put most of the creatures back in the pond, but we were allowed to take the tadpoles back to class.

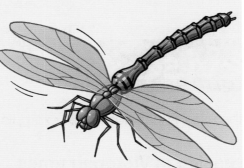

a. Draw a line like this **/** in the text to show where any new paragraphs should go.

b. Explain why you think the paragraph breaks should go there.

_____

_____

_____

c. Describe what each of your paragraphs is about.

_____

_____

_____

Headings and subheadings

What is a heading and subheading?

↺ Recap

Headings are titles for a whole piece of text. Subheadings are titles for sections or paragraphs of text. They tell you what the section is about. They help to organise information on the page and make it easier for the reader to find information.

🗐 Revise

Look at the use of headings in this example passage.

💡 Tip

Headings are usually in bold or bigger writing so that you can identify them easily. Sometimes they are underlined.

The seaside in Victorian times

Introduction
During Victorian times, the British seaside became a popular holiday destination. Families would take day trips to the beach. It was much less common to holiday abroad.

Punch and Judy
Punch and Judy was a famous puppet show performed for children on the beach.

Buckets and spades
Buckets and spades were used to build sandcastles just as they are today. However, the buckets and spades were made from metal and wood rather than the plastic used now.

The sea
The outfits people wore to swim in the sea were very different to the swimming costumes used today. Ladies wore swimwear that looked more like a dress and men usually wore an all-in-one garment that looked like long shorts and a T-shirt.

✔ Skills Check

1. **Read the passage above.**

   a. What are the four subheadings in the passage?

   _____ _____ _____ _____

   b. How do you know they are subheadings?

   _____

   c. Read the last paragraph. Explain why 'The sea' is *not* a good heading.

   _____

Word families

What is a word family?

↻ Recap

A **word family** is a group of words that are related and have a similar meaning. Word families are created by adding different prefixes and suffixes to a **root word**.

KEY WORDS
word families
root word

📋 Revise

Here is part of a word family based on the root word help: **helpful**, **helpfully**, **unhelpful**, **helpless**. Let's look at some more examples of root words and word families.

Root word	Word family
appear	disappear, reappear, appearance
cycle	tricycle, bicycle, cyclist, recycling
extend	extent, extensive, extension
medicine	medical, medicinal
nature	natural, unnatural, naturally
oppose	opposite, opposed, opposing
possess	possession, possessive
remember	remembrance, remembered

✔ Skills Check

1. Match these words to their word family by writing them in the correct column.

musical   electricity   legality   attentive   irregular

illegal   attention   regulate   electrician   musician

electric	music	attend	regular	legal

Prefixes

What is a prefix?

↺ Recap

A **prefix** is a set of letters added to the beginning of a word to turn it into another word. For example: un + happy = **un**happy

re + appear = **re**appear   dis + like = **dis**like

📄 Revise

The prefix **in** means the opposite. When a root word begins with certain letters, the prefix **in** changes.

in + active = **in**active   in + correct = **in**correct

im + mature = **im**mature   **im** + possible = **im**possible ← root word beginning with **m** or **p**: the prefix **in** becomes **im**

ir + regular = **ir**regular ← root word beginning with **r**: the prefix **in** becomes **ir**

il + legal = **il**legal ← root word beginning with **l**: the prefix **in** becomes **il**

The prefix **sub** means under.

sub + zero = **sub**zero

The prefix **inter** means among or between.

inter + national = **inter**national

✔ Skills Check

1. **Add a prefix to each word so that the new word has the opposite meaning. Write the new word in the box.**

Word	New word
patient	
responsible	
act	
legible	
marine	

💡 Tip

Most prefixes are added to the beginning of root words without any spelling changes.

KEY WORD

prefix

Don't forget that in might change to im or ir or il.

Suffixes

What is a suffix?

↺ Recap

A **suffix** is a word ending, or a set of letters added to the end of a word to change its meaning.

📝 Revise

Use the rules in the table to learn how to add suffixes correctly.

Suffix	Rule	Examples
ation	Add to the end of the word. If the root word ends in **e**, remove the **e** before adding **ation**.	inform + ation = inform**ation** ador**e** + ation = ador**ation**
ly	Add to the end of the word. If the root word ends in **le**, change it to **ly**. If the root word ends in **ic**, add **ally**.	sad + ly = sad**ly** gent**le** + ly = gent**ly** bas**ic** + ly = basic**ally**
ous	Add to the end of the word. If the root word ends in **our**, change it to **or** before adding **ous**.	poison + ous = poison**ous** hum**our** + ous = hum**orous**
ion	If the root word ends in **t** or **te** use **tion**.	act + ion = ac**tion** hesita**te** + ion = hesita**tion**
	If the root word ends in **ss** or **mit**, use **ssion**.	confe**ss** + ion = confe**ssion** per**mit** + ion = permi**ssion**
	If the root word ends in **d**, **de** or sometimes **se**, use **sion**.	exten**d** + ion = exten**sion**, deci**de** + ion = deci**sion** ten**se** + ion = ten**sion**
cian	When the root word ends in **c** or **cs**, use **cian**.	musi**c** + cian = musi**cian**

KEY WORD

suffix

✔ Skills Check

1. Change each word below by adding the suffix shown. Write the new word in the box.

Word	Suffix	New word
final	ly	
danger	ous	
politics	cian	

Word	Suffix	New word
dramatic	ly	
prepare	ation	
invent	ion	

Plurals

What is a plural?

↺ Recap

Plural means 'more than one'. **Singular** means 'only one'. There are rules for spelling plural words.

📋 Revise

For most words, to change a word from singular to plural, you add an **s** on the end. However there are a lot of exceptions to this rule! Here are some examples:

Tip

Watch out for the irregular plurals that don't follow the rules!

KEY WORDS
plural
singular
consonants

Add es
when the word ends in **ch, sh, ss, x** or **o**.

Singular	Plural
chur**ch**	chur**ches**
wi**sh**	wi**shes**
dre**ss**	dre**sses**
bo**x**	bo**xes**
potat**o**	potat**oes**

Add es and change y to i
when the word ends in **y** with a **consonant** before it.

Singular	Plural
par**ty**	par**ties**
butter**fly**	butter**flies**

Add es and change f to v
when the word ends in a **f** sound (including **ife**, where the final **e** is not the last sound)

Singular	Plural
hal**f**	hal**ves**
loa**f**	loa**ves**
kn**ife**	kni**ves**

Or
just learn these irregular plurals – they don't follow the rules!

Singular	Plural
tooth	teeth
foot	feet
person	people

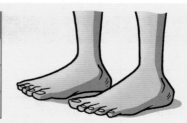

✔ Skills Check

1. Write the plural for each singular word below.

Singular	Plural
boy	
curtain	
pony	
ditch	
fish	
sheep	
class	
life	

2. Write the singular for each plural word below.

Singular	Plural
	wishes
	tomatoes
	plates
	feet
	foxes
	loaves
	kisses
	coins

3. Circle the spelling mistake in each sentence below. Then write the correct spelling in the box.

a. George put the knifes and forks on the table ready for lunch.

b. Rakhee watched the butterflys out of the window.

c. The childs went to the theatre to see a funny play.

Longer vowel sounds

↺ Recap

What do you mean by 'longer vowel sounds'?

A longer **vowel** sound is a single sound that is longer than the short vowels (**a, e, i, o, u**). They are written as a group of letters that contain a vowel. They can be tricky to spell as you can write the same sound in different ways.

Revise

Let's look at some examples of longer vowel sounds and how to spell them.

Vowel sound	Examples
air	fair, hair, pair
ear	bear, pear, wear, tear
are	fare, care, share, scare
ore	more, core, shore, tore
or	short, born, horse, morning
au	autumn, August, dinosaur
aw	crawl, yawn, dawn, draw, saw
ei	vein
eigh	weight, eight, neighbour
ey	they, obey
ough	although
ow	know, snow, grow

Can you think of any more ways to make some of these sounds?

💡 Tip

There are often several different ways to spell the same longer vowel sounds. Try to think of all the possibilities when you are spelling a word!

KEY WORDS

vowel

✔ Skills check

1. Circle the longer vowel sounds in these sentences.

air ear are	While we waited for my mum to have her hair cut, I shared a pear with my brother. We read a book about a big brown bear. We took it in turns to turn the pages so that it was fair.
ore or au aw	This morning I was drawing a dinosaur when, after a short time, my dad asked if I wanted more breakfast.
ei eight ey	My neighbours who live at number eight have a dog. He is taken for walks around the park. The dog doesn't obey his owners so they keep him on a tight rein.
ough ow	Although it had snowed heavily, school was still open. Later, the caretaker showed us where the melted ice was flowing down the hill.

2. Circle one spelling mistake in each sentence. Then write the correct spelling in the box.

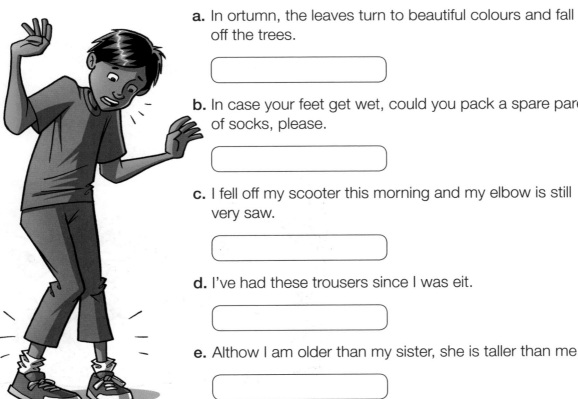

a. In ortumn, the leaves turn to beautiful colours and fall off the trees.

b. In case your feet get wet, could you pack a spare pare of socks, please.

c. I fell off my scooter this morning and my elbow is still very saw.

d. I've had these trousers since I was eit.

e. Althow I am older than my sister, she is taller than me.

Tricky sounds

What do you mean by 'tricky sounds'?

↺ Recap

Tricky sounds are letters (or groups of letters) that don't sound the same as they are spelled.

📄 Revise

Here are some tricky sounds and how to spell them.

Words	Spelling	Sound
scheme, character, echo	ch	k
chauffeur, parachute, moustache	ch	sh
discipline, fascinate	sc	s
century, centre, circle, pencil	c	s (sometimes called 'soft c')

Look at the tricky sounds highlighted in the examples below.

The noise e**ch**oed around the room.

Here the **ch** makes a **k** sound.

The para**ch**ute opened in time.

Here the **ch** makes a **sh** sound.

I was fa**sc**inated by the play.

Here the **sc** makes a **s** sound.

She drew a **c**ircle with a sharp pen**c**il.

Here the **c** makes a **s** sound.

A **c** before **e**, **i** and **y** often makes a **s** sound. Here are some more examples.

'c' makes a 's' sound before...		
e	i	y
century	city	cylinder
centre	circle	cycle
centipede	cinema	fancy
cancel	icicle	spicy
ice	pencil	icy

Tip

Words with tricky sounds like these often come originally from other languages, such as French, Greek or Latin. For example:

Spelling	Sound	Origin
ch	k	Greek
ch	sh	French
sc	s	Latin

✔ Skills Check

1. Sort these words according to the sound they make. Write them in the correct column.

came   centre   caterpillar   city   carry   cylinder   cycle   continue   candle   centipede

'k' sound	's' sound

2. Sort these words according to the sound they make. Write them in the correct column.

chemist   machine   chair   brochure   church   chocolate   chef   character   cheese

chorus   chalet   chaos

'ch' sound	'k' sound	'sh' sound

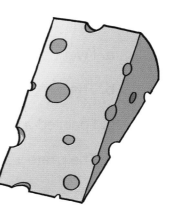

Tricky endings

↺ Recap

What do you mean mean by 'tricky endings'?

Tricky endings are word endings that sound the same, or very similar, but are spelled differently.

It can be easy to make mistakes with these words!

📄 Revise

Let's look at some examples of the tricky endings **sure**, **ture** and **(ch)er**.

Ending	Examples
sure	measure, treasure, enclosure, pleasure
ture	adventure, picture, furniture, creature
(ch)er	teacher, richer, catcher, stretcher

Tip 💡

You just have to learn how to spell these words, because you can't always tell the ending from the way they sound!

When you add **er** to a root word ending in **ch**, it sounds the same as (or very similar to) **ture**.

✔ Skills Check

1. Complete the unfinished word in each sentence with the correct ending.

> sure   ture   cher

a. I went on an exciting adven_____ .

b. The tea_____ handed out a sticker at the end of the day.

c. I painted a beautiful pic_____ .

d. The pirate was searching for trea_____ .

e. We went on a na_____ trail to find bugs and worms.

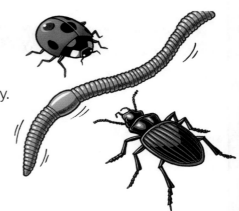

Homophones

What is a homophone?

↺ Recap

Homophones are words that sound the same but are spelled differently and mean different things.

📄 Revise

Here are some examples of common homophones.

fair	It's not **fair**. She has more sweets than me.
fare	The bus **fare** was £1.50.

style	He painted a picture in the **style** of a famous artist.
stile	We climbed over the **stile** on our walk in the countryside.

air	Mum opened the window to get some fresh **air**.
heir	The prince is **heir** to the throne.

alter	I need to **alter** my dress so it fits properly.
altar	There are beautiful flowers on the **altar** in church.

aloud	She meant to whisper, but she said it **aloud**.
allowed	I was not **allowed** to go to the party.

How many different examples of homophones can you list?

KEY WORD

homophones

✔ Skills Check

1. Circle the correct word to complete each sentence. Then write it in the space provided.

a. I had fish and chips for my _____ course at lunchtime. (**main / mane**)

b. She had to decide _____ she wanted blue or green trainers. (**weather / whether**)

c. The princess was _____ to the kingdom. (**air / heir**)

d. You need to _____ the cheese to make cheese scones. (**grate / great**)

e. He decided to _____ the end of the story as it was too sad. (**altar / alter**)

f. We had three turns each on the slide so it was _____ . (**fair / fare**)

Syllables and longer words

What is a syllable?

↻ Recap

A **syllable** is like a beat in a word. Longer words have more than one syllable. Breaking longer words down into syllables can help you to spell them.

📄 Revise

Using syllables is one way to help you remember how to spell longer words. Break the word into parts, say each part slowly and clearly and try to work out how to spell it.

Word	Syllables	Number of syllables
early	ear/ly	2
address	ad/dress	2
exercise	ex/er/cise	3
remember	re/mem/ber	3
separate	sep/a/rate	3
favourite	fav/ou/rite	3
experience	ex/pe/ri/ence	4
material	mat/e/ri/al	4
particular	par/tic/u/lar	4
accidentally	ac/ci/dent/al/ly	5

Clapping a word can help you work out how many syllables it has.

KEY WORD
syllable

💡 Tips

There are lots of ways to learn to spell longer words.

● Practise writing them – again and again!

● Write them in different ways and places. Try chalk outside or coloured icing on a plate.
  Or write a word in a long line, each time getting smaller and smaller. How many times can you write the word before it gets too small to write? For example:
  disappear disappear disappear disappear disappear disappear disappear disappear disappear disappear

● Pick six of your spellings and challenge yourself to use these words in a story.

✔ Skills Check

1. Write the number of syllables for each word below.

Word	Number of syllables
ordinary	
famous	
natural	
perhaps	
interest	
disappear	

2. Try writing some of these longer words. Read the sentence, look at the word, hide it, have a go at spelling it, then check to see if you were right.

Don't forget to cover up the word when you spell it!

Sentence	Word	Spell it
I **promise** I will tidy my room tomorrow.	promise	
You need to **complete** your maths homework by Wednesday.	complete	
There were **various** different cereals to choose from.	various	
Please **continue** with the story.	continue	
Imagine if dinosaurs were still alive today.	imagine	
We had **potatoes** for lunch.	potatoes	

Why not practise spelling some of the words on page 68?

Identifying and summarising main ideas

What does identifying and summarising main ideas mean?

Revise

Here are some of the main ideas to look for in different types of text.

Non-fiction	Fiction
What the text is about Important facts, taken from across the whole text	The main characters The setting Key events The conclusion

Here is a non-fiction text with the main ideas of each paragraph highlighted. This information is then sumarised below.

Dinosaurs

Dinosaurs lived on the planet millions and millions of years ago, before they mysteriously died out. There are several theories as to why dinosaurs became extinct, but no one really knows.

Scientists learn about dinosaurs by studying their fossils and bones. Scientists who study dinosaur fossils are called palaeontologists (pay-lee-on-tol-ogists). There were hundreds of different types of dinosaur.

Tyrannosaurus Rex (T-rex) was a ferocious meat-eating dinosaur. It had large, pointy teeth to crush through bones as it ate dinosaurs and other animals. It walked around on its two powerful legs and had two small arms. T-rex was an enormous dinosaur.

Triceratops walked on four legs and had a huge head with three horns on it. This is how it got its name, as the word *triceratops* means 'three-horned head'. Many scientists believe that the horns were used for protection from the meat-eating dinosaurs. These horns were up to a metre long.

Summary of main ideas

- The text is about dinosaurs.
- Palaeontologists study dinosaur fossils.
- T-rex was a ferocious meat-eating dinosaur.
- Triceratops had three horns on its head.

- Skim-read the text.
- Highlight main ideas from the text.
- Summarise your main ideas, with a few words or short sentences to explain them.
- If there is more than one paragraph, try to select a main idea from each paragraph.
- Use very few adverbs or adjectives – keep your summary short!

✔ Skills Check

1. a. Read the text below and underline the main ideas.

Reduce, reuse and recycle

A huge amount of waste material is produced in the United Kingdom. Most of this waste is taken to landfill sites and buried in the ground. This can be harmful for the environment.

Recycling means waste products are turned into something new, resulting in less waste ending up in landfill sites. Items that can be recycled include cardboard boxes, yoghurt pots and glass bottles and jars.

Reusing means using items again. For example, plastic bottles can be refilled with water, plastic bags can be used again and again to carry groceries each week, and yoghurt pots can be used as paint pots. Furniture and clothing can be sold or given to someone else who could use them.

Reducing waste involves using fewer materials in the first place. For example, take your own bag when you go shopping, and make sure you use food by its use-by date and don't throw it out unnecessarily.

b. Summarise the main ideas in this text.

_____

_____

_____

_____

_____

49

Identifying themes and conventions

↻ Recap

What are themes and conventions?

Themes are ideas that go through a text. Conventions are common features that tell you what type of writing it is.

Revise

Let's look at some of the features and conventions of different text types.

Text type	Examples	Conventions and features	Themes
Story	Fairy stories Traditional tales Fables Myths and legends Adventure stories Humorous stories Mystery stories	Characters and setting Beginning, middle, end Problem and solution Paragraphs Sometimes chapters	Good over evil Love and hate/friends and enemies Journeys or quests Wisdom and foolishness Heroism and bravery Morals (in fables) Mythical creatures (in myths)
Poem	Shape poems Limericks Sonnets Ballads Nonsense poems	Verses Capital letter to start each line Exploring and playing with words	Nature and animals Feelings and friendship Everyday happenings Epic tales Historical events
Recount	Diaries Newspaper articles Historical recounts	Past tense In time order Pictures/photos and captions	Personal life events Journeys and holidays News stories Historical events
Report	Information texts Explanation	Headings Paragraphs Pictures/diagrams/photographs Bullet points	Factual subjects (such as geography, science, history) Accurate/reliable information
Instructions	Recipes How to make…	Equipment list Numbered points Commands (put, chop, mix) Conjunctions of time (first, then)	Details of how to make things (such as food, crafts, toys, furniture)

✔ Skills Check

1. Read this text, then answer the questions below.

Theseus and the Minotaur

Theseus the Prince of Athens set sail on a warm, windy afternoon. He was sailing for the island of Crete. Theseus had bravely volunteered as one of the seven young men to be fed to the Minotaur every year. His quest was to defeat the furious, hungry Minotaur and free the people of Athens.

After a long journey, Theseus finally arrived at the island. He was taken to the complex maze beneath the castle of King Minos, where the Minotaur lay waiting for his meal. While Theseus fearlessly prepared for his mission, a princess appeared and gave him a ball of string.

Theseus used the ball of string to lay a trail behind him as he walked through the confusing maze of tunnels. He could smell the horrid stink of the Minotaur, an evil creature with the head of a bull and the body of a man.

Theseus heroically killed the creature and then followed his trail of string back to the entrance.

a. What type of text is this? Tick **one**.

Instructions ☐   Myth ☐   Poem ☐

b. What is the creature called? _____

c. Who is the hero? _____

d. What is the hero's aim?

_____

_____

e. Which theme can you see in this text? Tick **one**.

Journeys or quests ☐   Wisdom and foolishness ☐

Love and hate ☐

Retrieving and recording information

What does retrieving and recording mean?

Retrieving information means finding the information you need from a text to answer questions.

Recording information means writing it down.

📄 Revise

See if you can spot the answers in the text.

Look at the example questions below. You can look for key words in the passage that are in the question to help you, they have been highlighted below.

1. Read this text, then answer the questions below.

Milk

Milk can be produced by cows or goats. It is a highly nutritious white drink and is also used to produce lots of different foods, such as cheese, butter and yoghurt. These foods are called dairy products.

Dairy farmers milk cows using a milking machine. The milk is then cooled in large tanks to keep it fresh. Often, the milk is collected in special vehicles called milk tankers which take the milk to a large dairy. At the dairy the milk is treated to kill any bad bacteria and to make sure it is safe to drink. This is called pasteurisation.

 Milk contains calcium which is important for helping our bodies to develop strong, healthy bones and teeth. It also contains other vitamins that help us to grow and stay healthy. Milk can be enjoyed as part of a healthy diet on its own or in other foods.

a. Which food product is created from **milk**? Tick **one**.

Lettuce ☐   **Cheese** ✓   Crisps ☐

b. What name is given to the foods **produced** from **milk**?

These foods are called dairy products.

c. What is **pasteurisation**?

Pasteurisation is when milk is treated to kill any bad bacteria.

d. Why is **calcium** good for our bodies?

Calcium helps our bodies to develop strong, healthy bones and teeth.

Tips

- Read the text and questions carefully.
- Skim-read the text again to find the answers.
- Use the text to help you find and write the answer.
- Re-read your answer to check that it answers the question.

Think about what the question is asking you to do.

✔ Skills Check

1. Read this text, retrieve the information you need and record your answers below.

Rocks

There are three main types of rock. These are igneous, metamorphic and sedimentary rocks.

Igneous rocks are formed when magma is forced from the earth in a volcano. As the magma cools, it forms rocks. Examples include basalt and granite. Granite is very practical and has many uses, including paving stones, kitchen worktops and gravestones.

Sedimentary rocks are formed from sediments such as other tiny rocks and animal skeletons pressed together in layers. Examples include chalk, clay and sandstone. These are softer rocks. Chalk can be used to draw with.

Metamorphic rocks are rocks that have changed from another type of rock due to heat and pressure. Examples include slate and marble. Slate is often used for roof tiles.

Now read the questions and have a go at finding the answers in the text.

a. How many different types of rock are there? _____

b. What can granite be used for? Give two examples from the text.

_____

c. Which rock can be used to draw with? Tick **one**.

Marble ☐   Basalt ☐   Chalk ☐

d. How are metamorphic rocks created?

_____

Making predictions

How do you make predictions?

↻ Recap

Making predictions means saying what you think will happen next using evidence from the text.

📝 Revise

Read this text. What happens next? Some clues have been highlighted that help you predict.

Megan's friend Noah had come round to her house after school.

"Wow! Can we play with that?" asked Noah, pointing to a small remote control car up on the shelf.

"Oh, I'm not sure, Noah. **It's really fragile and it was my dad's when he was a little boy,**" explained Megan, **looking worried.**

"It's OK, I'll be careful," said Noah as he pulled it down off the shelf. **Tossing the car onto the floor,** he started pressing buttons and pulling levers on the controller. The little car was sent **whizzing off towards the wall.**

"No! Gently! One lever at a time," shouted Megan as she watched the old toy car **spinning round in circles.** Then suddenly…

What do the clues tell us?

"I'm not sure"/looking worried these suggest that Megan thinks it is not a good idea, and something bad could happen.

"It's really fragile… it was my dad's when he was a little boy" shows that it could break easily, it belongs to someone else, is old and perhaps precious.

Tossing the car onto the floor suggests that Noah is not being careful at all.

Whizzing off towards the wall/spinning round in circles implies that the car is out of control.

So the clues suggest that the toy car gets damaged or broken in some way. Now we can use these clues to make a prediction, give a reason for it and explain the evidence.

prediction ⟶

reason

explanation of clues in the text ⟶

I think that the toy remote control car gets badly damaged because Noah is being careless with it and the toy goes out of control. The text says Noah tossed the car onto the floor and that it was whizzing and spinning round. Megan is also worried which suggests something bad could happen.

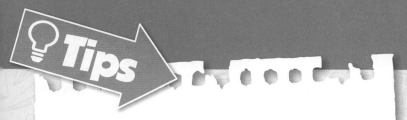

- Underline clues in the text.
- Give a reason for your prediction.
- Explain what the clues are telling you.

✔ Skills Check

1. Read this text, then answer the questions below.

A new bike

Ollie had a new bike for his birthday. It was shiny and blue and he was really proud of it. That morning, his mum asked him to go to the shop and buy some bread, as they had run out.

Ollie cycled past two older boys sitting on the wall opposite the shop.

"Nice bike," one of the boys whispered to the other and nodded in Ollie's direction. They looked like they were up to something and made Ollie feel nervous.

Outside the shop Ollie looked in his rucksack for his bike lock, but he had forgotten it. At first, he couldn't decide what to do. His mum would be cross if he didn't get the bread and you weren't allowed to take bikes into the shop, so he left his bike and ran into the shop.

When Ollie came out of the shop, the boys across the road had gone and so had his bike.

a. What do you think happened to Ollie's bike?

_____

_____

b. Use evidence from the text to explain your answer.

_____

_____

_____

_____

Making inferences

↻ Recap

Sometimes an author doesn't tell you everything in a text. You have to use clues in the text to work out what is happening. This is called making inferences.

🗒 Revise

In this example, the author does not simply write: 'Oliver was nervous about going horse riding'. Instead, she suggests this, by describing Oliver's behaviour.

evidence that suggests Oliver might be feeling nervous →

Oliver was at the stables. He was about to go for his first riding lesson **since he had fallen from a horse.** He was wearing his riding hat and riding boots. Oliver watched as Maya put the saddle on **the huge horse.** As he watched, his **hands got all sweaty,** his **face went pale** and his **eyes grew wider.** Oliver **stepped slowly back, away from the horse.**

"Come on Oliver, on you get," said Maya cheerfully.

Oliver didn't move.

Now you can use the evidence in the text to explain what you have inferred about Oliver's behaviour. For example:

Oliver's hands got all sweaty, his face went pale and his eyes grew wider suggests that he is feeling nervous and scared.

The horse was huge and Oliver had not been riding since he fell off are reasons *why* he might be scared.

Oliver backed away from the horse and wouldn't get on when Maya asked him to shows that he didn't want to go.

This is fun – it's just like solving a puzzle!

Tips

- Read the text carefully.
- Highlight the evidence (clues) in the text.
- Use the evidence from the text to support and explain your answer.

It can be helpful to underline the clues you find in the text.

✔ Skills Check

1. Read this text, then answer the questions below.

> Farah sat at the dinner table. Everyone else had finished eating. Farah's plate sat in front of her. She had eaten everything *except* the peas. Farah stabbed a pea onto the end of her fork and slowly lifted it to her mouth. She made a face before the pea even touched her lips.

Do you think Farah likes peas? Circle **one**.

　　Yes　　　　No

Explain your answer, using evidence from the text.

_____

_____

2. Read this text, then answer the questions below.

> Ali was going to a music concert and had been waiting for the tickets to arrive. He ran to the door when he heard the post drop through the letter box and onto the floor. Picking up the post Ali searched through the letters until he found them! His tickets had finally arrived. Ali ripped open the envelope and pulled out the colourful music concert tickets. A huge smile spread across his face.

How is Ali feeling about going to the music concert?

_____

Explain how you know.

_____

_____

_____

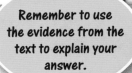

Remember to use the evidence from the text to explain your answer.

57

Language features

↻ Recap

What are language features?

Language features are things that writers use to make their text more interesting.

📋 Revise

This table summarises some important language features to look out for.

Language feature	Description	Examples	The effects are to...
Choice of words	Interesting words: ● adjectives ● adverbs	**delicious** cake **cute**, **furry** mouse **Suddenly**, the door banged open.	● make a text more interesting ● create a picture for the reader
Rhyming words	When word endings sound the same	**map**, **tap**, **clap**, **zap**, **date**, **mate**, **crate**, **late**	● make a text easier to remember and fun to read aloud ● make phrases stand out ● add rhythm/beat and help it to flow
Repeated sounds	When words begin with the same letter or sound	**S**lowly, the **s**nail **s**lithered across the path.	
Words that describe sounds	When words sound like the sounds they describe	**bang**, **beep**, **boom**, **clap**, **clang**, **clip-clop**, **flap**, **moo**, **pop**, **splash**, **spit**, **toot**, **zip**	● create a sound image of the setting/event and bring it to life

💡 Tip

Look for different language features in a text and think about *why* the author used that feature. This will help you to explain what effect the feature has on the text.

✔ Skills Check

1. Read this text, then answer the questions below.

It was the middle of the day in the school holidays. Jane slept peacefully until her mother pulled back the curtains and a sea of light flooded the room. Slowly, Jane sat up and stretched. "Was it really time to get up already?" she asked herself. A bee buzzed noisily around the room. Once she was dressed, Jane poured herself a glass of fabulously fresh fruit juice.

a. Find a word that describes a sound in the picture.

_____

b. What effect does this have?

_____

c. Find an example of repeated sounds in the text.

_____

d. Which adverbs are used in the text? Write them below.

_____

e. What does 'a sea of light flooded the room' mean?

_____

_____

Words in context

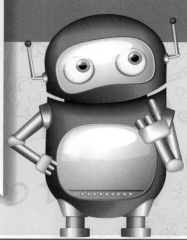

What are words in context?

Sometimes when you are reading, you come across a word that you don't understand. You need to use the clues in the text (the context) to work out the meaning.

📄 Revise

Some words have more than one meaning and you need to work out which meaning is meant.

Word	Meaning	Alternative meaning
row	line of something	to row a boat
light	opposite of dark	not very heavy
trip	journey	to fall over
duck	type of bird	to bend/lower your head
squash	fruit drink made with water	to squeeze/crush
date	dried fruit	day on a calendar
lift	elevator	to pick up
flat	somewhere to live	level/smooth

Some words even have three or more meanings! For example, squash is also a ball game played with rackets.

Some words you might not know at all and you need to work it out using the text.

1. What does the word 'harmoniously' mean in this sentence? Tick one.

Owen and Evie went to the sports centre. They hired rackets and a ball. They played squash **harmoniously**. They had lots of fun.

happily ✔   heroically ☐   nastily ☐

In this case, you should tick happily as it links best with 'fun' in the next sentence.

✔ Skills Check

1. What does the word 'flat' mean in this sentence? Tick one.

> We live in a flat in the centre of town.

Level ☐   Somewhere to live ☐   Smooth ☐

2. Which word has a similar meaning to 'swung' in this sentence? Tick one.

> I stood back as my brother swung the golf club at the little white ball.

waved ☐

moved ☐

bashed ☐

3. a. What does the word 'expedition' mean in this text? Tick **one**.

> At the weekend, I went on an expedition to the seaside.
> We travelled for several hours down the motorway.
> Finally, we arrived at the seaside where we had ice
> cream and built sandcastles.

memory ☐   journey ☐   entrance ☐

b. What evidence in the text tells you this?

_____

_____

Presentational features: non-fiction

↻ Recap

Texts can be presented in different ways, called presentational features. They give clues about what type of text it is, highlight important parts of the text and even affect its meaning.

Revise

Here are some examples of presentational features in non-fiction texts.

Feature	Purpose	Effect
Bold writing	To highlight words and headings	They may change the emphasis the reader puts on these words in a sentence. When used in headings, they help the reader know what the text is about.
Italics	To add emphasis or show that something is important	
Underlining	To make a title, heading or subheading stand out, or to emphasise a word	
Headings/ subheadings	To label paragraphs or sections of text	They help direct the reader to the right section of the text.
Paragraphs	To break the text into sections	They make the text easier to read and understand by organising the content into sentences linked by a theme.
● Bullet points or 1. Numbered points	To summarise the text or to order parts of it	These help the author to highlight the key points/facts for the reader. Numbered points tell the reader in what order to complete a task, which may be important to get the best results.
Pictures/ photographs/ diagrams	To show what something looks like, or give visual clues	Images give the reader a clear visual picture to add to the writing. Captions tell the reader what the picture is for and what it shows
Captions	To label pictures or photographs	
Layout	To enhance the effectiveness of the text. For example: newspaper articles – in columns, large headings instructions – numbered points	This helps the reader to identify the text type and purpose, and to get the most out of the text.

✔ Skills Check

1. Read this text, then answer the questions below.

1 [ ]

2 [ ]

3 [ ]

4 [ ]

→ ## Fruit kebabs

→ **Ingredients**
- 200g strawberries
- pineapple
- large bunch of green grapes
→ - banana
- 100g milk chocolate
- 12 wooden kebab sticks

Fantastic fresh
fruity kebabs

5 [ ]

Method

1. First, wash the strawberries and remove the stalks.

2. *Carefully*, use a sharp knife to cut the pineapple into 2cm cubes.

3. Peel and slice the banana.

4. Then thread the fruit onto the kebab sticks, one at a time. Use about 6 pieces of fruit on each stick, and try to create a repeating pattern with the fruit you choose.

5. After that, slowly melt the chocolate in a microwave.

6. Dip the fruit kebabs in the melted chocolate and then place them on greaseproof paper on a tray.

7. Finally, put the tray of kebabs in the fridge for about 30 minutes to allow the chocolate to set.

a. Use the features below to write labels in the numbered boxes around the text.

subheading   heading   bullet points   caption   picture

b. Why is the word 'Carefully' in italics?

_____

c. Why are the sentences in the **Method** numbered?

_____

Presentational features: fiction

↻ Recap

Fictional texts (such as poetry, stories and comic strips) have their own presentational features. Poetry in particular uses a wide variety of features to help the reader explore language on the page.

📄 Revise

Here are some examples of presentational features in fiction texts.

Text type		Feature	Effect
Story	Paragraphs	These organise the story into sections	This makes it easier for the reader to follow the text.
Poetry	Font style	This changes the shape and appearance of the letters	These can be used to emphasise the meaning of a word. For example:
	Font size	Individual words/phrases can be bigger or smaller	*wobble* The baby was really tiny.
	CAPITAL LETTERS	These show that words are loud or being shouted	The reader can shout when reading aloud to add surprise. For example: "BOOM went the big bass drum!"
	Shape	Poems can be written in different shapes around or across the page	This can add meaning and interest to a poem. For example, a poem about a tower might be written as a vertical list.
	Length of lines	Lines in a poem can be very short or very long	This changes the flow of a poem and can make it short, snappy and fast, or slow and gentle.
Playscripts	Bold text	The character names are often bold and spaced out from the spoken text	Makes it easier for the reader to identify the characters.
	Italic text	Stage directions are often in italics to show what is happening	Tells the reader what the characters are doing to give them direction.

Tips

Presentational features can make the text look fun and exciting!

The layout, presentational and language features of a text can add meaning and emphasise text, as well as adding interest to the look of the text on the page.

✔ Skills Check

1. Read this poem, then answer the questions below.

Long, extended, lengthy snake. Slithering, sliding, gliding snake. Powerful, strong, deadly snake <

a. Why do you think the poet has written the poem like this?

_____

_____

b. How has the poet used presentational features to create the snake's head?

_____

_____

2. Read this playscript, then answer the questions below.

Red Riding Hood is skipping through the wood holding a basket and bumps into the wolf.
Red Riding Hood: Hello Mr Wolf.
Wolf: Why, hello little girl. What are you doing on this fine day?
Red Riding Hood: I'm off to see my grandmother to give her this basket of food.

a. Which presentational features are used in this text? Tick **two**.

Bold writing ☐   Speech bubbles ☐   Italics ☐   Subheadings ☐

b. How does the stage direction help the reader to understand the text?

_____

_____

Glossary

A

adjectives are sometimes called 'describing words' because they pick out features of nouns such as size or colour. They can be used before or after a noun. The red bus.

adverbs can describe the manner, time, place or cause of something. They tell you more information about the event or action.

adverbials are words or phrases that give us more information about an event or action. They tell you how, when, where or why something happened.

apostrophes:
- show the place of missing letters (**contraction**)
- show who or what something belongs to (**possession**).

C

clauses are groups of words that must contain a subject and a verb. Clauses can sometimes be complete sentences.
- A **main clause** contains a subject and verb and makes sense on its own.
- A **subordinate clause** needs the rest of the sentence to make sense. A subordinate clause includes a conjunction to link it to the main clause.

commas have different uses, including:
- to separate items in a list
- to separate a fronted adverbial from the rest of the sentence
- to clarify meaning.

common nouns name something in general (boy, man).

conjunctions link two words, phrases or clauses together. There are two main types of conjunction.
- **co-ordinating conjunctions** (and, but) link two equal clauses together.
- **subordinating conjunctions** (when, because) link a subordinate clause to a main clause.

consonants are most of the letters of the alphabet except the vowel letters a, e, i, o, u.

contraction a shortened word with an apostrophe to show show the place of missing letters

co-ordinating conjunctions (and, but) link two equal clauses together.

D

determiners go before a noun (or noun phrase) and show which noun you are talking about.

direct speech is what is actually spoken by someone. The actual words spoken will be enclosed in **inverted commas**: "Please can I have a drink?"

E

exclamation marks show the end of exclamations and some commands.

F

fronted adverbials are at the start of a sentence. They are usually followed by a comma.

full stops mark the end of statements.

H

homophones are words that sound the same but are spelled differently and mean different things.

I

inverted commas are punctuation used with direct speech: "Please can I have a drink?"

M

main clause contains a subject and verb and makes sense on its own.

N

nouns are sometimes called 'naming words' because they name people, places and things. A **proper** noun (Ivan, Wednesday) names something specifically and starts with a capital letter. A **common** noun (boy, man) names something in general.

noun phrases are phrases with nouns as their main word and may contain adjectives or prepositions. Enormous grey elephant/in the garden.

P

past tense verbs describe past events. Most verbs take the suffix ed to form their past tense.

perfect form of a verb usually talks about a past event and uses the verb have + another verb. **Past perfect**: He had gone to lunch. **Present perfect**: He has gone to lunch.

phrases are groups of words that are grammatically connected so that they stay together, and that expand a single word. Phrases do not contain a subject or a verb.

plural means 'more than one'.

possession a word using an apostrophe to show who or what something belongs to.

prefix is a set of letters added to the beginning of a word in order to turn it into another word.

prepositions link nouns (or pronouns or noun phrases) to other words in the sentence. Prepositions usually tell you about place, direction or time.

present tense verbs describe actions that are happening now.

progressive or 'continuous' form of a verb describes events in progress.
- **present progressive:** We are singing.
- **past progressive:** We were singing.

pronouns are short words used to replace nouns (or noun phrases) so that the noun does not need to be repeated.
- **personal pronouns** replace people or things.
- **possessive pronouns** are used to show who something belongs to.

proper nouns name something specifically and starts with a capital letter (Ivan, Wednesday).

Q

question marks show the end of questions.

R

root word is a word to which new words can be made by adding prefixes and suffixes: happy – unhappy – happiness.

S

singular means 'only one'.

subordinate clause needs the rest of the sentence to make sense. A subordinate clause includes a conjunction to link it to the main clause.

subordinating conjunctions (when, because) link a subordinate clause to a main clause.

suffix is a word ending or a set of letters added to the end of a word to turn it into another word.

syllable sounds like a beat in a word. Longer words have more than one syllable.

T

tense is **present** or **past** tense and normally shows differences of time.

V

verbs are doing or being words. They describe what is happening in a sentence. Verbs come in different tenses.

vowel sounds are made with the letters a, e, i, o, u. Y can also represent a vowel sound.

W

word families are normally related to each other by a combination of letter pattern, grammar and meaning: child – children – childish – childlike.

Word lists These are the words you need to learn to spell.

Years 3–4

accident	difficult	interest	potatoes
accidentally	disappear	island	pressure
actual	early	knowledge	probably
actually	earth	learn	promise
address	eight/eighth	length	purpose
answer	enough	library	quarter
appear	exercise	material	question
arrive	experience	medicine	recent
believe	experiment	mention	regular
bicycle	extreme	minute	reign
breath	famous	natural	remember
breathe	favourite	naughty	sentence
build	February	notice	separate
busy/business	forward/forwards	occasion	special
calendar	fruit	occasionally	straight
caught	grammar	often	strange
centre	group	opposite	strength
century	guard	ordinary	suppose
certain	guide	particular	surprise
circle	heard	peculiar	therefore
complete	heart	perhaps	though/although
consider	height	popular	thought
continue	history	position	through
decide	imagine	possess	various
describe	increase	possession	weight
different	important	possible	woman/women

Answers: Year 4

Page 6

1   **a.** The <u>astronauts</u> prepared for their <u>journey</u> to (Mars.)
    b. (Ms Green) gave the <u>class</u> their <u>homework.</u>
    c. The <u>doctor</u> used a <u>stethoscope</u> to listen to (Amelia's) <u>heart</u>.
    d. The <u>tourists</u> visited (Buckingham Palace) in (London.)
    e. "My <u>birthday</u> is in (June)," said (Hannah) excitedly.

Page 7

1   Any 'interesting' adjective that makes sense in the sentence. For example:
    a. huge, gigantic, massive, enormous
    b. ancient, decaying, historic, shabby
    c. delicious, tasty, yummy, mouth-watering

2   Any adjectives (one or more, before either or both nouns) used/combined in a way that makes sense in the sentence. For example:
    a. owl: wise, old, magnificent, white, powerful, beautiful
    branch: long, strong, skinny, crooked, drooping
    b. cyclist: old, young, fit, fast, slow, wobbly, colourful, famous
    lane: bumpy, narrow, wide, winding, twisty, country
    c. teacher: old, new, grumpy, friendly, horrid, lovely, strict
    hall: old, new, sports, grand, huge, small

Page 8

1   unhelpful, incomplete, irresponsible

2   Any answer that implies the prefix 'un' has the opposite (or negative) effect on the word.

Page 9

1   **a.** <u>The lonely, frightened evacuee with a suitcase</u> stood on the platform.
    b. The robin is stood on <u>the broken, empty bird-bath by the path</u>.
    c. The children played happily in <u>the soft, yellow sand near the dunes</u>.
    d. Amber borrowed <u>the only English dictionary in the library</u>.
    e. Omar took <u>the last apple muffin on the tray</u>.

Page 11

1   **a.** We **swam** at the outdoor pool in town.
    b. He **wrote** a letter of complaint.
    c. The frog **jumped** out of the pond.

2

Sentence	Verb type
I have drawn a picture.	Past tense
I am drawing a picture.	Present tense
I draw a picture.	Past progressive
I was drawing a picture.	Present progressive
I drew a picture.	Present perfect

3   **was playing   was cooking**

4   The princess **has rescued** the prince from the tower.

Page 13

1   **a.** Sadly   **b.** sometimes   **c.** downstairs
    d. yesterday   **e.** Suddenly

2   Any adverb that makes sense in the sentence. For example:
    a. Yesterday, Happily
    b. loudly, angrily
    c. Later, Tomorrow
    d. sleepily, comfortably
    e. Carefully, Gently, Quickly

3   Any suitable adverbs. For example:
    a. unexpectedly, today, yesterday, upstairs
    b. outside, outdoors, happily, excitedly, carefully
    c. Happily, Now, Regularly, Sometimes, Consequently

Page 14

1   **a.** I went to the park <u>last Thursday afternoon</u>.
    b. We waited for our drinks <u>in the sunshine</u>.
    c. The little girl ran to the finishing line <u>as fast as she could</u>.
    d. The children were playing football <u>all morning</u>.
    e. The enormous dog barked <u>in the garden</u>.

Page 15

1   **a. In assembly,** Ms Wilkinson played the piano.
    b. Suddenly, the bell rang.
    c. At the end of break time, we went inside.
    d. Along the beach, the woman walked her dog.

Page 17

1

	Main clause	Subordinate clause
I washed my hands **after I went to the toilet.**		✓
When I lost my favourite teddy, I was upset.		✓
I jumped when the door slammed loudly.	✓	
Before I went on stage, **I was feeling nervous.**	✓	
I shut the window when it rained.	✓	
The lights went out **because the power was cut off.**		✓

2   **a.** <u>The girl walked to school</u> although it was raining.
    b. <u>The bus was late</u> because it broke down.
    c. As it was snowing, <u>the football match was cancelled</u>.

3   **a.** He cleaned out the guinea pigs <u>after feeding the rabbit</u>.
    b. <u>When we were younger</u>, we went ice-skating with our grandma.
    c. <u>If I go on Saturday</u>, I will see the animals at the zoo.

Page 18

1   **a.** She put sun cream on <u>before</u> she went outside.
    b. I have two brothers (so) I know lots about football.
    c. You can have raisins (or) you can have grapes.
    d. <u>If</u> you cook dinner, I'll do the washing up.

Page 19

1   **a.** a   **b.** your

2   **a.** The boy ate **an** orange for his lunch.
    b. Please can I have **some** peas?

Page 21

1   **a.** They   **b.** I   **c.** his   **d.** She her   **e.** she her

2   **a.** she   **b.** he   **c.** its   **d.** they   **e.** he his

Page 22

1   **a.** after   **b.** during   **c.** beside   **d.** under

2   **a.** School was closed **because of** the snow.
    b. I had to eat all my carrots **before** pudding.
    c. The snake was curled **around** a branch of the tree.

PUNCTUATION

Page 23

1 a. **U**sually in **O**ctober, the leaves fall off the trees.
b. **L**ily and **M**eg visited **E**dinburgh **C**astle, on their school trip.
c. **T**he new pilot, who was called **T**om, often flew to **G**ermany.

2 No. Capital letters are also used for proper nouns (such as names of people and places).

Page 25

1 a. When it rains, our garden is full of puddles.
b. Any answer that suggests: This sentence is a statement so it needs a full stop.

2 a. When can I go outside to play**?**
b. When it rains hard, we have break time inside**.**
c. Pick that up**.** (or **!**)
d. What an amazing feeling**!**

3 It was the school holidays**.** Jessica and Nathan were out walking in the woods when they came to a broken bridge. "How annoying!" cried Nathan. "How are we going to get across the stream now**?**" thought Jessica. They both looked at the fast-flowing stream and the slippy rocks underneath the broken bridge**.** It was no good, they would have to walk downstream until they found a safe place to cross.

Page 26

1 a. doesn't He's   b. can't I'll

2

Words in full	Contraction
you had/would	you'd
are not	aren't
should have	should've
he will	he'll

Page 27

1 a. children**'s**   b. bridesmaids**'**   c. babies**'**   d. boys**'**

Page 29

1 "Look at all that rain!" exclaimed Grandad. "I think we will have to go in the car today."

2 Charlie was standing at the end of the dinner queue.
"I am so hungry!**"** he moaned.
"Me too. Why are we always last?**"** said his friend Sam.
"I just hope there is some chocolate cake left,**"** replied Jing, who was just in front of Charlie.
Then the lunchtime assistant told them, **"**You don't need to worry. There's plenty of cake for everyone.**"**

Page 30

1 He used flour, sugar, butter and eggs to make a delicious cake.

2 a. For breakfast, I had pancakes**,** yoghurt**,** fruit and honey.
b. On sports day, she competed in the egg and spoon race**,** the skipping race and the obstacle race.
c. In the film about nocturnal animals there were owls**,** bats and foxes.

Page 31

1 a. Before school**,** I had a swimming lesson.
b. Last year**,** my teacher was Mr Davies.
c. At the weekend**,** her aunt came to visit.

2 a. **In January**, it snowed and snowed.
b. **Yesterday afternoon**, I went to the museum.
c. **At the airport**, we had to sit and wait for Granny's plane.
(The comma must be present and in the correct place.)

Page 33

1 a. Two clear lines (**/**): one between 'its head.' and 'After that'; one between 'in class.' and 'When we'.
b. Any answer that suggests: the topic changes each time.
c. first paragraph: dragonflies; second paragraph: flatworms; third paragraph: what the children did with the creatures they had found

Page 34

1 a. Introduction, Punch and Judy, Buckets and spades, The sea
b. They are in bold (and on a separate line).
c. Any answer that suggests: The sea is mentioned but the paragraph is not mainly about this.

VOCABULARY

Page 35

1

electric	music	attend	regular	legal
electricity electrician	musical musician	attention attentive	irregular regulate	illegal legality

Page 36

1

Word	New word
patient	**impatient**
responsible	**irresponsible**
act	**interact**
legible	**illegible**
marine	**submarine**

Page 37

1 finally, dangerous, politician, dramatically, preparation, invention

SPELLING

Page 39

1

Singular	Plural
boy	boys
curtain	curtains
pony	ponies
ditch	ditches
fish	fish/fishes
sheep	sheep
class	classes
life	lives

2

Singular	Plural
wish	wishes
tomato	tomatoes
plate	plates
foot	feet
fox	foxes
loaf	loaves
kiss	kisses
coin	coins

3 a. knives   b. butterflies   c. children

Page 41

1

air ear are	While we waited for my mum to have her h**air** cut, I sh**are**d a p**ear** with my brother. We read a book about a big brown b**ear**. We took it in turns to turn the pages so that it was f**air**.
ore or au aw	This m**or**ning I was dr**aw**ing a dinos**au**r when, after a sh**or**t time, my dad asked if I wanted m**or**e breakfast.
ei eight ey	My n**eigh**bours who live at number **eigh**t have a dog. He is taken for walks around the park. But the dog doesn't ob**ey** his owners so th**ey** keep him on a tight r**ei**n.
ough ow	Alth**ough** it had sn**ow**ed heavily, school was still open. Later, the caretaker sh**ow**ed us where the melted ice was fl**ow**ing down the hill.

2 a. autumn   b. pair   c. sore   d. eight   e. although

Page 43

1 **'k' sound:** came, caterpillar, carry, continue, candle
   's' sound: centre, city, cylinder, cycle, centipede

2 **'ch' sound:** chair, church, chocolate, cheese
   'k' sound: chemist, character, chorus, chaos
   'sh' sound: machine, brochure, chef, chalet

Page 44

1 **a.** I went on an exciting adven**ture**.
   b. The tea**cher** handed out a sticker at the end of the day.
   c. I painted a beautiful pic**ture**.
   d. The pirate was searching for trea**sure**.
   e. We went on a na**ture** trail to find bugs and worms.

Page 45

1 **a.** main   **b.** whether   **c.** heir
   d. grate   **e.** alter   **f.** fair

Page 47

1
Word	Number of syllables
ordinary	4
famous	2
natural	3
perhaps	2
interest	3
disappear	3

2 Check the children's answers.

READING

Page 49

1 **a.**
   A huge amount of waste material is produced...
   ...waste is taken to landfill sites...
   ...harmful for the environment.
   Recycling means waste products are turned into something new...
   Reusing means using items again...
   Reducing waste involves using fewer materials in the first place...
   b. Main points from the text, brief and concise, covering all 4 paragraphs. For example:
   • Huge amounts of waste in UK
   • Waste taken to landfill sites/harmful to environment
   • Recycling turns waste into something new
   • Reusing uses things again
   • Reducing uses less to start with

Page 51

1 **a.** Myth   **b.** The Minotaur   **c.** Theseus
   d. To kill the Minotaur/survive the maze
   e. Journeys or quests

Page 53

1 **a.** Three
   b. Any two: paving stones, kitchen worktops, gravestones
   c. Chalk
   d. Metamorphic rocks are created when one type of rock changes to another due to heat and pressure.

Page 55

1 **a.** It was stolen.
   b. An answer including any of the following clues:
   The boys outside the shop looked suspicious.
   The boys were whispering about the bike.
   Ollie didn't lock the bike.
   The boys had gone and so had the bike.

Page 57

1 No. Answers must refer to evidence in the text. For example, the text says:
   • she ate everything *except* the peas, which suggests she didn't like them
   • she lifted one pea slowly to her mouth/she made a face when she went to eat the pea, which suggests she didn't want to eat it.

2 **a.** Excited/happy (or similar)
   b. Answers must refer to evidence in the text. For example, the text says:
   • he ran to the door and searched the post/ripped open the tickets, which suggests he couldn't wait
   • he smiled when he saw the tickets, which suggests he was very pleased/happy.

Page 59

1 **a.** buzzed
   b. Any answer that suggests:
   It describes/gives a picture of the sound.
   c. bee buzzed/fabulously fresh fruit
   d. peacefully, slowly, really, already, noisily, fabulously
   e. Any answer that suggests:
   The sunlight filled the room (like water flooding a container).

Page 61

1 Somewhere to live

2 moved

3 **a.** Journey
   b. Answers must refer to evidence in the text. For example, the text says they went on a coach and travelled for a long time to the seaside.

Page 63

1 **a.** (1) heading, (2) subheading, (3) bullet points, (4) picture, (5) caption
   b. To emphasise the word/make the word stand out
   c. Any answer that suggests:
   The numbers show the order in which to carry out the steps.

Page 65

1 **a.** Any answer that suggests:
   It creates a shape similar to what the poem is about – a snake./The shape of the poem (a long line) emphasises the meaning and words in the text.
   b. Any answer that suggests one or both of the following:
   • The word 'snake' is bigger and in bold.
   • The red '<' looks like a forked tongue.

2 **a.** Bold writing, italics
   b. Any answers that suggest the following: it helps the reader/the actors know what the characters are doing as well as what they are saying.

Revision planner

Grammatical words

Revised **Achieved**

☐	☐	Proper nouns and common nouns	6
☐	☐	Adjectives	7
☐	☐	Adjectives with prefixes	8
☐	☐	Noun phrases	9
☐	☐	Verb tenses	10
☐	☐	Adverbs	12
☐	☐	Adverbials	14
☐	☐	Fronted adverbials	15
☐	☐	Clauses	16
☐	☐	Conjunctions	18
☐	☐	Determiners	19
☐	☐	Pronouns	20
☐	☐	Prepositions	22

Punctuation

Revised **Achieved**

☐	☐	Capital letters	23
☐	☐	Full stops, question marks and exclamation marks	24
☐	☐	Apostrophes for contraction	26
☐	☐	Apostrophes for possession	27
☐	☐	Inverted commas	28
☐	☐	Commas in lists	30
☐	☐	Commas after fronted adverbials	31
☐	☐	Paragraphs	32
☐	☐	Headings	34

Vocabulary

Revised **Achieved**

☐	☐	Word families	35
☐	☐	Prefixes	36
☐	☐	Suffixes	37

Spelling

Revised **Achieved**

☐	☐	Plurals	38
☐	☐	Longer vowel sounds	40
☐	☐	Tricky sounds	42
☐	☐	Tricky endings	44
☐	☐	Homophones	45
☐	☐	Syllables and longer words	46

Reading

Revised **Achieved**

☐	☐	Identifying and summarising main ideas	48
☐	☐	Identifying themes and conventions	50
☐	☐	Retrieving and recording information	52
☐	☐	Making predictions	54
☐	☐	Making inferences	56
☐	☐	Language features	58
☐	☐	Words in context	60
☐	☐	Presentational features: non-fiction	62
☐	☐	Presentational features: fiction	64